I WHALE ALWAYS LOVE YOU

W. Books

I love you BEARY much

Anyfin is possible when we're together. You're simply

FIN-TASTIC!

It's not a

STRETCH

to say you mean everything to me

I love to give you

HEDGE-HUGS!

There's nothing like spending

KOALA-TY

time together

To be honest,
I'm bananas for you
And i'm not

MONKEYING

around!

I will

OWLWAYS

be by your side

You're so

SEAL-LY!

I love HANGING with you!

You are

TOADALLY

amazing!

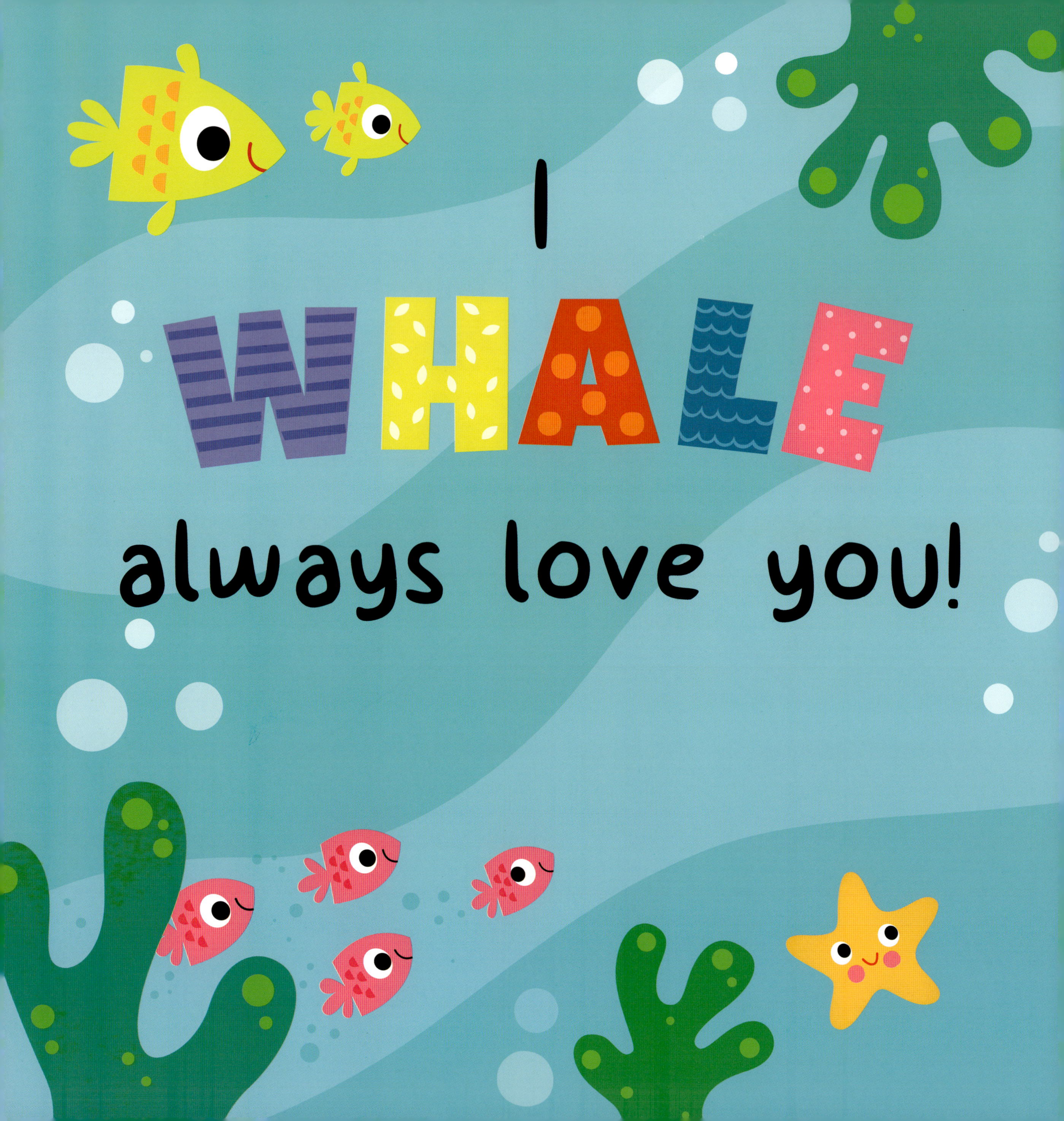

I WHALE always love you!